How to Sell Your Home for Top Dollar in ANY Market, ANYWHERE!

By Derek Bauer

The Only Real Estate Playbook
You'll Ever Need

Printed in the United States of America

First Printing, August 2012
ISBN 978-1478299967

Table of Contents

"Failing to plan is planning to fail" –
Ancient Proverb

Chapter One: The Pre-Game Warmup

For most of us, including me, rocket science is neither easy, nor simple. Selling a house, however, may not always be easy, but it is actually relatively simple.

Money is and always will be attracted to difference, yet real estate is a sea of "sameness." It IS possible to get more for your home…but not without doing more.

If you are a serious seller, and if you incorporate the concepts and principles outlined in this short, fun, easy read, you will very likely net more money than you would by putting a "For Sale By Owner" sign on a post in your front yard, or by calling someone who sells real estate to "put your home on the market."

All you need to do is follow the "5 Ps" that are outlined in this playbook and have a market expert in your corner. By implementing these 5Ps – plan, prepare, price, package, and persevere – you will drastically increase your odds of winning when it comes to the sale of your house! I'll show you how to leverage each of these principles in the chapters that follow.

Add a reputable real estate expert who is on top of their game to the mix and the odds that you'll net the highest price that the market will bear, and within a reasonable timeframe, will go up exponentially.

The playbook that you're reading right now summarizes some of the key points I have learned during my first 10 years in the real estate business. I believe these key concepts will stand the test of time and the advancement of technologies (but make no mistake that your real estate expert's incorporation of the latest technologies are KEY to your success), and should remain the core foundational principles of selling a home for top dollar, regardless of the current market conditions.

My goal with this book is to help you do just that while giving you the highest return possible on the investment in your house. I want you to realize the greatest yield, advance to the new phase of your life, and do so with a smile on your face. You can achieve all of these goals by implementing the strategies covered in this playbook. If you have plans to sell your home within the next 12 months, this playbook was either a wise investment or a valuable gift.

After years of working with sellers to implement these strategies and hearing from my clients that I was the first to make these exact recommendations to increase their net, I decided that it was time that the home-owning population learned the secrets that I've been using for over a decade. Now, some real estate agents may joke that their competitors do just three things when they list a home:

1) They Place a sign in the yard
2) They Put the house in the MLS
3) They Pray that an agent comes along to sell their listing

I hope that the agent you select goes *above and beyond* for you and that these tasks only scratch the surface of what should be an aggressive marketing plan to get your home sold at the highest possible price that the market will bear.

Our home selling team, for example, implements a 77-Point Marketing Strategy that covers all of the bases and more when it comes to marketing our clients' homes. For that strategy to be as effective as possible, however, we always start with the 5 Ps mentioned in Chapter One: plan, prepare, price, package, and persevere. It's a simple strategy that works every time.

Les Brown once said, "Someone's sitting in the shade today because someone planted a tree a long time ago." After years of working with sellers and continually hearing, "Oh you are the first person to have told us that", or "I wish we had known this when we sold properties in the past," I decided to pay forward some of the valuable knowledge I've learned along the way.

These are strategies that I implement in my own business daily – that's how strongly I feel about their value. I truly believe that these "5 Ps" will stand the test of time. In fact, I hope that decades from now someone learns something new from this playbook. I hope that nugget of knowledge creates an opportunity for them – or, for someone who is close to them.

As you go through this playbook you'll learn the key points and the process that you should follow in order to get the highest amount of money from your house and within the shortest timeframe possible. This isn't rocket science. In fact, as I mentioned earlier in this book, it will require work, focus, and possibly an investment, but it will be worth every bit of it!

From this playbook you'll also gain mid-level knowledge that is neither too general nor too specific. I won't get into granular detail on ideal paint colors for your walls, or what the best plants are for that window box that you're going to buy to help spruce up your house. I won't make recommendations on fixture metals. These are talking points that your REALTOR® and chosen staging professional will address with you. As proven experts in their fields, these professionals will help maximize return with knowledge, experience, and honest selling advice.

What you also won't find in this playbook is fluff or filler. I don't get too technical, nor do I delve into deep, complex, boring topics that you probably don't have the time or energy for anyway. All I can promise you is a fun, light read that's easy to grasp. I'll introduce you to concepts that anyone looking to maximize his or her property's monetary position can implement.

You can read this book in an afternoon or browse through it at your leisure. Come back to it often, share it with friends, family members, and co-workers and use it to attain the highest yield for the sale of your property – and in any market! [Please note: individual results may vary. That's why it is imperative to have the right experts in your marketplace ... who subscribe to the same principles in this playbook ... walking side-by-side with you so the right moves are made to win the game.]

"It takes as much energy to wish as it does to plan." -
Eleanor Roosevelt

Chapter Two: Plan

You might not believe this, but there is a market for your home in any economy and at any time. That's because there are always first-time buyers, and "move up" and "move down" buyers: people in smaller homes want bigger ones, people in mid-sized homes want large ones, people in large homes want to downsize, and renters want to start lining their own pockets (instead of their landlords'). It's just a part of the economic circle and one that you, as a homeowner, can tap into.

Before you put your home on the market you'll want to ask yourself these questions:

1. Why am I selling my house?
2. What are my goals with this sale?
3. How serious am I about selling?
4. What will I do if my home doesn't sell within a reasonable timeframe?
5. Are we going to be better off somewhere else?
6. Could we change something here in order to

stay and enjoy or tolerate?
7. What are our financial constraints, boundaries, guidelines, and limitations with this?
8. What would happen if we weren't able to get the number we wanted/needed?
9. What is the list of top reasons to move? To stay?
10. Is a move critical to employment, enjoyment, or both?
11. If we moved, what are the absolute "musts" for the next place?
12. If we moved, what are the absolute "nots" for the next place?
13. If the house didn't sell, how would that affect the plan/direction?
14. What would you miss if you moved?
15. What would you seek if you moved?

The answers to these questions will help you determine your motivations for selling and will serve as a valuable component of your overall sales plan.

Working Ahead

Determining your selling motivations in advance is important because some homeowners think they want to move, and then they realize that their current living conditions are tolerable enough and they stay put. Maybe your neighbor has an annoying dog that barks all night, or maybe your current home is too far of a commute from your job. Or it could be that you're tired of the landfill view from your kitchen window, or the golf balls from the adjoining course breaking your car windows. Oftentimes homeowners move because they need or want more space, and when adding on may not be the best financial move. Again, this is where the advice and counsel of a real estate expert will be helpful to you.

So let's say you love your house, its location, and the floor plan. You have a private yard and a sunroom that's blanketed in warm rays every morning. The most gorgeous park in the city is down the street and you're a runner who visits it often. Basically, you have a dream home that's got just a few, tiny quirks.

The question is: should you sell? From what I've seen during my career it's not uncommon for a homeowner to pick up and move for the wrong reasons. In fact, it happens all the time.

The house goes up for sale but the homeowners weren't committed to the process. They didn't – as motivational author Stephen Covey says – start with the end in mind. One day the dog next door barked incessantly at the mailman and bam! It was time to sell the house. There was no thought given to one of the most important Ps on the list: plan.

These scenarios often lead to disappointment and, even worse, can result in poor judgment and unfortunate decisions. Sometimes a homeowner sees this and takes the home off of the market. Some evergreens are planted to hide the landfill, and the dog next door becomes tolerable. "Life is good, so we will just stay where we are," the homeowners think to themselves.

> To avoid wasting time and energy on a sale that you aren't 100 percent committed to, you must first understand your WHY, and then try to figure out your WHAT.

Knowing exactly why you want to sell – and then making sure the reasoning is valid – can go a long way in helping you get that "Just Sold" rider on the For Sale sign that's in your yard. Furthermore, it will help you make better decisions when you are staring at the nuts and bolts/dollars and cents aspect of this transaction and transition.

Figuring out your motivations for moving also helps you determine just where you stand on the "serious scale." Putting a home on the market just to see if you can get a pie-in-the-sky price for it may have worked in the early-2000s, and people do test this strategy out in some markets (some may even succeed at it). This playbook is for the serious home seller and not the one who is flippant about testing the waters.

Selling a home and moving to a new property is a life-changing event for most people. The exceptions are transient individuals, families that are used to being uprooted regularly, or those who enjoy constant change (like many of my clients do). Moving is disruptive for many and not something that you may want to be doing every handful of years.

Moving a household for the wrong reasons can lead to other issues. The grass, as they say, is <u>not</u> always greener on the other side of the fence. For example, selling a home that's in good condition and/or in a great location just to secure a "great deal" on a new property for some equity opportunity may or may not be the best move. This is not always the best decision, especially if it means giving up a good combination of variables including: location, an enjoyable setting, schools and friends your kids enjoy and benefit from, and a floor plan that you love.

As you learned from this chapter, it's best to take the time to go through the planning stage and figure out your motivations first...before you put that sign in your yard.

"By failing to prepare, you are preparing to fail." –
Benjamin Franklin

Chapter Three: Prepare

Now let's look at a few things you can do to get ready for the
selling process. This stage comes after you answered your
WHY, and when you are ready to get down to brass tacks and
answer the HOW. This is a critical phase that a lot of
homeowners skip in their quest to get their homes onto the
MLS as quickly as possible. They don't ask HOW and they
don't take the proactive steps necessary to net the best price
possible – as opposed to a "viable" price – and within a
reasonable timeframe.

But you're different. You're going to go through the
preparation phase and set yourself up for success in the
market. The good news is that you won't have to go it alone.
There are professionals out there who are ready to help you,
counsel you, and share their opinions with you. Real estate
agents, brokers, title companies, appraisers, attorneys, and
others are standing by, ready to assist.

Here are the six critical steps that you'll want to take during
the "Prepare" phase of the home-selling process:

1. Make a list of the key characteristics that you feel are important to you when hiring a real estate expert. If you are unsure of what to look for, you'll find a good guideline in the chapter I wrote for the book, *The New Rise in Real Estate: The Nation's Trusted Real Estate Advisors Reveal Their Top Secrets for Buying and Selling Homes in the Real Estate Economy.*

2. Interview up to three top real estate experts in your area. If you don't know any personally, I can help. REALTORS® use nationwide, reputable, referral networks and that's exactly what I'll use to point you to experts in your area. If you want to work with the best of the best, visit the following website and we'll get you connected: ***www.RealEstateExpertLocator.com.***

3. Interview and identify a home staging professional who will come in

and make your abode shine. Your real estate expert should be able to recommend one, or you can find one through associations like the Accredited Staging Professional (**www.StagedHomes.com**) and the International Association of Home Staging Professionals (**www.iahsp.com**). The sites include lists of stagers in your area who will prepare your home for sale with the goal of making the property appealing to the highest possible bidder.

4. Tour your property with a stager and review his or her recommendations with your REALTOR®. Ask your agent what he or she thinks about the proposed changes and how they will help elevate your home's value in the buyers' eyes.

5. Choose your agent carefully. Select your agent based on his or her honesty, ethics, passion, skill sets, marketing ability, track record, business and negotiating acumen, organization, reputation, communication style, and support team. Do not pick your agent based on his or her estimated value of your property, unless that agent is planning to purchase the house (in which case that opinion is actually very important!)

6. Do a cost benefit analysis. This is an evaluation method that estimates the value of projects to determine whether they are worth undertaking or continuing. The calculation will help you determine which modifications or enhancements will be worth it by comparing cost to the expected return. This is an important exercise that you can work through with your REALTOR® to determine which investments will pay off and which ones won't.

The expert that you hire to sell your home should be able to cover all of these bases. When coupled with the 5 Ps outlined in this book, you'll be able to develop a can't-lose sales plan for your property. As a seller, you want to get the highest possible price that the market will bear via the most exposure feasible. You want this to happen as quickly as possible, with the fewest issues and by relying on sound communication throughout the process.

> Find an agent who will provide quick follow-up for prospects who are interested in your home while also handling the fine details of the process – from sign-up to sign-down.

There are more than 2 million people nationwide who have licenses to sell real estate, of which over 1 million of them belong to the National Association of REALTORS® (NAR). Only NAR members are entitled to use the term "REALTOR®."

NAR members must adhere to a strict Code of Ethics. By joining NAR, individuals have access to a wide range of classes, seminars, and certification opportunities. Local REALTOR® groups are active in community matters, and individual members are routinely involved in neighborhood organizations.

In essence, local REALTORS® are community experts. They track real estate trends, share neighborhood concerns, and participate in local matters. They're good neighbors who are in the business of helping others buy and sell homes. This is exactly the type of professional who should be working on your side during the home-selling process.

The National Association of REALTORS® advises homeowners to ask the following questions when interviewing REALTORS®:

What services do you offer?
What type of representation do you provide? (There are various forms of representation in different states. Some brokers represent buyers, some represent sellers, some facilitate transactions neutral parties, and in some cases different salespeople in a single firm

may represent different parties within a transaction.)

What experience do you have in my immediate area?

How long are homes in this neighborhood typically on the market? (Be aware that because all homes are unique, some will sell faster than others. Several factors can impact the amount of time a home remains on the market, including changing interest rates, local economic trends, location, and other variables beyond your control.)

What is your pricing strategy? Ask about recent market and sales activity. It's okay if you speak with several REALTORS® and their price estimates differ. Just be sure to ask how their price opinions were determined and why they think your home would sell for a given value. It's important to understand that a pricing strategy must go beyond just looking at "comps," as many agents call them. To be effective, your expert must also look at trends, absorption rates, and other key factors that we'll cover later in this playbook.

What is your marketing plan for my home? At listing

presentations, brokers will provide a detailed summary of how they market homes, what marketing strategies have worked in the past, and which marketing efforts may be effective for your home. The expert you select must have a rock-solid marketing plan for your property.

What happens if another REALTOR® locates a purchaser? That is, who will that broker represent, and how will he or she be paid?

What disclosures should you receive? State rules require brokers to provide extensive agency disclosure information, usually at the first sit-down meeting with an owner or buyer.

How long do you want to list your home? A "listing" agreement is a contract that shows the broker's obligations and outlines the terms under which your home is being made available for sale. The length of the agreement is a negotiable matter.

Successful Home Staging

There are some reasonable and powerful steps you can take to ensure that your home is in "showing shape" 24/7, and regardless of whether you need the help of a staging professional or not. Barb Schwarz, The Creator of Home Staging® and CEO at Stagedhomes.com, says the way you live in your home on a regular basis, and how you live in it while it's listed for sale, are two different things.

Here are some basic tips that sellers can use to keep their homes in showing condition, even if they are living in the home. Understand that the buyers must be able to mentally "move" into their new home. Make it easy for them to do this by keeping your home clean, uncluttered, and attractive inside and out.

After we examine some basic concepts of staging we will dig deeper into some concepts, examples, and even a video of improvement project results that my team and I have accomplished over the years.

INSIDE:

1. Remove any clutter from furniture in all rooms of your home. "Keep decorative objects on the furniture restricted to groups of 1, 3, or 5 items," advises staging expert Barb Schwarz, CEO at Stagedhomes.com.

2. Clear out those kitchen countertops. Put away anything that you don't use regularly.

3. Remove any pictures and magnets from the refrigerator. An empty-but-clean kitchen gives buyers the freedom to envision their own possessions in the space.

4. Take a look around the bathrooms and remove any unnecessary clutter from the tubs, showers, and countertops. You can leave out the items that you use every day, but try to keep even those to a minimum.

5. Coordinate bathroom towels to one or two colors to create an attractive space.

6. Go through the common areas of your home and remove all unnecessary furniture and other bulky items that are taking up space. It's not unusual for a room to be overcrowded with furniture, but it is in your best interest as a seller to create a good balance of furniture and empty space.

7. Look at the pictures and other artwork on walls and in other places in your home. Remove any that don't make the room as attractive as possible.

8. If you remove pictures from the walls, be sure to patch and paint any holes.

9. Give every room of the house a thorough review and then paint, patch, clean, and replace as needed.

10. If your possessions must be stored during the showing period, rent some space at the local mini-storage.

11. Keep the home as light as possible. Open curtains and blinds during the day and always leave lights on during showings.

12. Have appropriate mood music on during the day for all viewings.

OUTSIDE:

1. Move all trashcans, materials, and other unsightly items into the garage.

2. Sweep and clean out the roof gutters.

3. Trim back all trees and other foliage so that it is at least a few feet away from the home.

4. Keep the yard trimmed and mulch all planting areas to create a "fresh" look from the curb.

5. Clear out decks, patios, and pool areas from personal items. Put them in the garage or in the mini-storage unit until the home is sold.

6. Capitalize on curb appeal by putting a fresh coat of paint on the front door and placing a new welcome mat at the entryway.

The good news is that in most cases home staging requires more labor than money. From my business, we have taken 10 properties and prepared a video example that you can watch at **www.StagingResults.com**. These transformations have netted our clients a great deal of money! For instance, we've had many clients change countertops from laminate to granite or another solid surface. Such changes have produced a return of 500 percent or even more in some cases. These are projects that need to be handled smartly, though.

The addition of a kitchen tile backsplash and under-cabinet lighting can work wonders and – when combined with professional photography and professional video – ensures that you're ready to WIN and get a return on that investment you made for your kitchen to pop!

Replacing tired and worn laminate with fresh materials is often a wise move, even if it is just a higher-end laminate that looks like ceramic tile (or whatever is relevant and desirable in your market at the time). Do what others won't and remember that people will pay for difference, not similarity.

You will be amazed at what some fresh paint coupled with the right accessories will accomplish. These small touches go a long way in making a home presentable for sale and ready to show to the market. Also, many stagers offer furniture, accessories, pictures and other items that you can "rent" during the marketing process.

Here are some key pointers that Rob Leece with Sensible Home Staging shares with homeowners who want to get the highest returns from their staging investments:

- Interview potential stagers to make sure your personalities are compatible.

- Look for a stager who can tell you the truth about your house and give you a perspective from the buyer's viewpoint.

- Ask for three references: one real estate agent and two staging clients.

- Find out if the stager is accredited by a national home staging professional association. For example, Stagedhomes.com defines the ASP (Accredited Staging Professional) designation this way, "Accredited ASP Stagers are true professionals trained under strict guidelines using proven staging techniques developed for over 30 years."

- To create a finely-staged home, ask yourself:

  a. Will buyers view the home as "move-in ready?" (Buyers will pay a premium for a move-in ready house.)
  b. Does the staging highlight the key features of the home? (Highlight the fireplace with colorful artwork or the deck with a sisal rug underneath your seating area to ensure buyers appreciate your home's features.)

c. Does the Staging create the "Wow" factor and emotional appeal needed to get an offer? (You have 30 seconds when the buyer walks in the front door to create that first impression.)

If you are working on a limited budget, focus on these key staging strategies:

- Update the kitchen and bathrooms. This provides the best return on investment.

- Install granite and under-cabinet lighting to create a custom kitchen.

- Replace the bathroom faucets and place a silk orchid on the vanity.

- Create a resort/spa-like look in your master suite.

- Update your bedding with bright bold patterns; add fresh white towels and nautical features to the master bath.

- Modernize the light fixtures throughout the house with "Pottery Barn®" dark iron metal finish fixtures. Make sure the lighting is consistent in every room.

- Focus on cleanliness: the house should look and smell clean. Freshly painted walls in a warm neutral color will impress buyers. Don't necessarily paint the ceilings white. Pick a lighter version of the wall color to warm up the space.

- Get a basic home inspection to ensure you won't have any last minute surprise expenses or seller concessions.

- You can also include a copy of the home inspection with your house details to give buyers a sense of security that the house is well maintained.

"The best advice I can give home sellers is to view the process of selling your house as a business transaction," says Leece. "Ask your REALTOR® to provide two listing prices that your house will sell for. First, list price in that you do no updating and list as is. Second you invest in updating and making it move in ready."

With seven years of staging experience under his belt, Leece says updating your house will help you will sell faster and for more money. He also points out that the selling process can be stressful for your family, particularly when it comes to keeping the house maintained and clean for showings.

"Like you, I don't like strangers going through my house and looking in all my drawers and personal belongings," Leece points out. "Investing in staging and updates to the house will result in selling it faster and will reduce your stress levels."

Here are Leece's final tips for home sellers:

- Every house has a personality or style, keep that in mind when you stage the property. If the house is mid-century modern, use furniture and accessories that highlight that style.

- Replace all CFL green energy bulbs with high-watt natural light bulbs.

- Invest in large, oversized artwork. Purchase something you like and that you can take to your new place.

- Bring in the natural light. Open all window blinds/curtains for showings. Clean the inside/outside of your windows so they sparkle. (Don't forget the basement windows.)

- Remove all personal hygiene items from the shower. Place items on vanities you might find in a hotel, like plants and soap baskets.

- Don't forget to clean out the basement and the garage. Use self-storage to move out the stuff we all collect over the years. Buyers want to ensure they have enough storage for their stuff.

Ideally, your stager will use as many of your current belongings as possible when rearranging furniture, de-cluttering, adding accessories, cleaning, and so forth. In many cases staging requires more labor then it does money, which is a great thing!

Many stagers offer furniture, accessories, and more to rent for the period it takes to get the home sold and closed. This is a case-by-case scenario: one home may be in obvious need of staging, whereas another may not need as much help in this area. Lean on the professionals you are hiring for their expertise with this and you'll be able to get the most out of your staging investment.

By the Numbers

You'll get the lowdown on home pricing in the next section of this playbook, but for now it's important to understand that your real estate professional should generate, provide, and explain the data necessary to come up with an effective price for your home. Some of the data he or she should provide and decipher for you includes:

Average days on market (DOM)
Absorption rates
Pricing quartiles
Neighborhood and community real estate activity
Pricing trends
List-to-sales price figures/data
The property's current condition
Which homes failed to sell

Months supply of inventory

Some of this data is also available online and free to the public. We encourage you let the experts gather, review, and explain the information to you, and to create a market snapshot that you can refer to regularly.

You can use the information to determine exactly where your home stands in the scheme of things, how much competition it currently has, how long it will likely be on the market, and what price you'll be able to get for it.

Your REALTOR® can also help you *interpret* the data – something you may not be able to do (or, may not want to do) on your own. He or she will help you make sense of it all and apply that knowledge to your specific situation.

REALTORS® who have their thumbs on the pulse of the market and multiple sales under their belts can draw conclusions and help you understand the market in plain English. They'll also help you grasp the value of home staging and home improvements, and explain how these strategies impact sales prices.

Looking Beyond the Web

There's a reason why more than 85 percent of homebuyers work with REALTORS® even after starting their home searches on the web. It's because the real estate deal itself is complex and having a pro in your corner can mean the difference between success and failure.

The same holds true for home sellers who need more than just a website to estimate the sales prices of their homes. An investment in a top-shelf agent will generally net a homeowner more than the commission itself, thanks to the agent's marketing ability and creativity in finding qualified buyers.

> Top agents get competing offers and use their negotiating ability to keep the seller's interest at the forefront. They also use business processes and customer service methods centered on their client: you.

Remember that your goal is not to just find <u>any</u> REALTOR® to list your home. Your goal is to find a stellar pro who knows the market and who has an excellent track record with exemplary statistics and the results it will take to win. Don't just settle for the first real estate agent who flashes a nice listing presentation in front of you. Get referrals from friends, find out which agents in your area are selling the most homes, and do your homework.

You can also check out your local or state REALTOR® association's website (most have a Find a REALTOR® section) or by visiting one of the myriad sites that allow consumers to rate agents. Look at your local media (TV, newspaper, radio) to see who is in the news, or take the easier route and visit **www.RealEstateExpertLocator.com** to let us connect you with two experts in your area to select from. These experts implement our strategies in order to get you top dollar within a short period of time.

REALTORS® are in the trenches every day. They know how buyers think, how to show properties, and how to position a home for optimal exposure. Because it's in their best interest to see your transaction through to the closing table, REALTORS® do what it takes to get your property sold – and to get you into a new home (either by selling it to you themselves, or by working with a referral network across the U.S.) as quickly as possible.

Ideally the real estate professional you choose will have a selection of reputable, qualified, service providers for you to pick from. He or she should be able to provide one or two good prospects for all disciplines, including staging.

Now that you know what goes into the preparation phase of the home-selling process it's time to dig down a little deeper and look at one of the most important components of any sale: price.

"Price is what you pay. Value is what you get." –
Warren Buffet

Chapter Four: Price

Before you start to pinpoint a specific price for your home, look around at your own market. What's it like right now? Are prices appreciating, depreciating, or stabilized? Are sellers getting what they want for their homes or are they dropping their asking prices multiple times before sealing the deal?

The initial price of your home is so crucial that it deserves its own chapter in this playbook. Much like the initial planning and preparation phases, this is a step that you won't want to gloss over. Take the time to work with your REALTOR® to come up with a viable price – or risk watching your home languish on the market for months or years on end, and realize that too high of an asking price can and will likely cost you money.

The latter is something you want to avoid at all costs since buyers who see 100 to 200+ days on the market can literally *sense* desperation on the seller's part. This is not a situation that you want to be in as someone who is using the 5Ps to get the best price in the least amount of time!

> To figure out a price, start by
> looking at the deal through the
> eyes of the would-be buyer.
> Would <u>you</u> pay the price that you
> have in mind? Why or why not?
> (We know it's your pride and joy,
> but try to be objective here.)

Let's assume for a moment that you live in an area where the real estate market is appreciating (home prices are increasing on a regular basis every quarter). Let's also say that you worked with your REALTOR® to come up with a home value of $250,000. Before you put that number in the local Multiple Listing Service (MLS), consider the fact that your home's value will likely increase to $260,000 within a few months. Is it smart to list it at $250,000 and also let the market know the price will rise to $265,000 in 45 days?

Probably, and here's why:

> You <u>will</u> likely get some competing offers at your desired price – or beyond – because that figure, albeit at a premium now, will look good six months from now to the buyer who had the foresight to predict that increase.

Now, things work the opposite way in a depreciating market. Where you may have some leeway when it comes to overpricing in an appreciating market, the same doesn't hold true when home values are retreating. The idea that "we can always come down in price" doesn't work at all in these types of markets, and in fact it is a liability as an approach in any market. Have you ever chased a ball downhill? It's not easy, is it? That thing just keeps rolling faster and faster, thanks to momentum, and you can't get your hands on it until it hits bottom. This is not the analogy that you want to emulate when selling your home!

A better approach is to work with your REALTOR® to come up with a sales price that the market will bear, given the current selling conditions. So if that value is $250,000, and if prices in the area are dropping at a rate of 1% to 2% every 30 days, then you can get out ahead of the market by pricing your home at $245,000.

This will help you "catch" buyers instead of chasing after them. It isn't possible to under-price a property; the market won't allow it. A great price will result in competition in demand, which will in turn be reflected in a higher sales price.

Here's how the logic works:

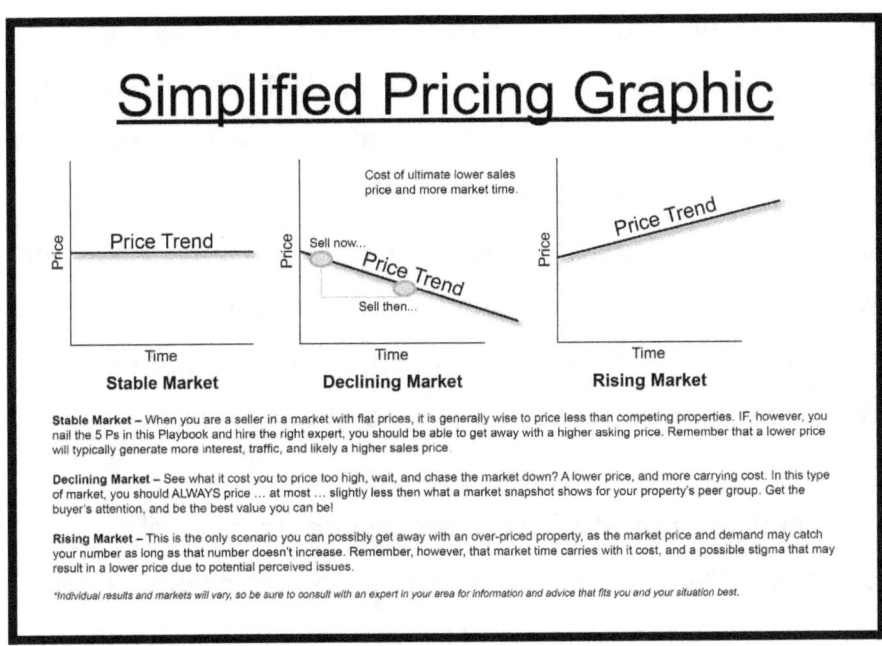

Simplified Pricing Graphic

Stable Market – When you are a seller in a market with flat prices, it is generally wise to price less than competing properties. IF, however, you nail the 5 Ps in this Playbook and hire the right expert, you should be able to get away with a higher asking price. Remember that a lower price will typically generate more interest, traffic, and likely a higher sales price.

Declining Market – See what it cost you to price too high, wait, and chase the market down? A lower price, and more carrying cost. In this type of market, you should ALWAYS price ... at most ... slightly less then what a market snapshot shows for your property's peer group. Get the buyer's attention, and be the best value you can be!

Rising Market – This is the only scenario you can possibly get away with an over-priced property, as the market price and demand may catch your number as long as that number doesn't increase. Remember, however, that market time carries with it cost, and a possible stigma that may result in a lower price due to potential perceived issues.

Individual results and markets will vary, so be sure to consult with an expert in your area for information and advice that fits you and your situation best.

A true real estate expert can guide and counsel you on the best pricing strategy. He or she knows the latest market trends, understands buyer motivations, and has a keen interest in getting your home sold as quickly as possible and for top dollar. Now, if you can't find a top-producing agent in your market we would be happy to help you. Please visit **www.RealEstateExpertLocator.com** and we will give you a choice of several good agents to select from in your area.

Beware of Pricing Assumptions

You may be wondering why pricing is so critical right out of the gate. After all, you are thinking to yourself, if I price it too high at first I can just drop it down as needed. While this strategy may work at a garage sale, it's not effective in the real estate market, where the newest listings generate the most excitement. To leverage that excitement you should put your home on the market only when it is truly ready to sell (and not when half of the kitchen floor is torn up and in need of replacement) and only at the most appropriate price.

The market – not you or your real estate agent – will determine the price of your house. Using the collaborative efforts outlined in this playbook you'll be able to drive the market activity. The market will respond with what it "feels" the price of your home should be. Using the steps we've laid out, you'll be able to create a package that appeals to the market and that sells for the highest possible price.

> All real estate ultimately sells for market value and you need to influence that value as much as possible.

Instead of controlling the sales process you will find yourself chasing the market. This is an expensive way to sell a home, especially if you are located in a declining or depreciating market. Overprice a home in an appreciating market and you may be able to survive that move as prices rise, but you will still face the potential stigma of too much market time.

Extended market time is a red flag for homebuyers. The home that languishes on the market for months will always have a stigma attached to it. Think of it this way: it's human nature to want what others want, and so it remains true that most don't want what others didn't want. You don't want your home to fall into the second category.

Skip the critical steps outlined in this chapter and you'll essentially take the wind out of the sails you have worked so hard to raise, and you'll miss out on those crucial first two to three weeks on the market. During that time your property will appear on the radar screens of buyers and agents who have been actively searching for the right home, but who haven't found it yet.

Overprice your home and it will quickly fall off of those radar screens as buyers and agents look elsewhere. Your home will become yesterday's news. Even if you successfully implement the rest of the advice in this book, pricing your home incorrectly will result in much wasted investment and effort.

This is the time to be extremely observant and engaged in the sale of your home. It's also the time to avoid agents who focus only on what your property is worth (unless they are going to buy your property!). The market is what it is, and a great agent will implement the strategies outlined in this book to get top dollar for your home within the shortest timeframe. Pricing will play a big role in making that happen because the market ultimately determines what it will pay. The more of the market that sees and is impressed with what your home offers, the higher the sales price will ultimately be.

Here's how it works:

If a property is priced too high, it doesn't get showings.
If a property is priced above market, it gets showings, but no offers.
If a property is priced correctly, it has substantial interest and

will field multiple offers.
If you overprice your home by 10%, you will likely see at least a 90% reduction in showings and a 5% over-price will likely result in a 70% reduction in showings.
Less traffic equates to fewer offers. That means more market time, and ultimately a lower sales price coupled with increased costs.

As we stated earlier, it really is not possible to under-price a property because the market will not allow it. For example, we recently priced a property at $175,000 and in just four days we had nine offers with an ultimate sales price of $189,000. Had we priced it even at $185,000, it very likely would not have sold at that level, given my experiences. Missing the mark on this one will take money out of your pocket.

As a seller, your goal is to make sure that multiple buyers want your home at the same time. Competing interest and bids are the true way to set market value. For instance, if you and your agent determine that a reasonable buyer would pay $250,000 for your property, you may likely net more money by pricing it at or slightly below that figure then by knowingly overpricing it.

You'll use this strategy even if you aren't in a rush to sell (if this is you, please revisit the first chapter of this playbook to determine if you are a serious seller or not). Throwing your home on the market for six months to "see what happens" could come back to haunt you down the road when you really want or need to sell. Buyers will see that no one wanted your home at the time, so why should they want it now?

The Price is Right

The Internet has put a lot of information into the hands of potential buyers and sellers. The number of online sources that publish sales and market data grows by the day. Because many of these sources pull from public records and don't account for numerous necessary variables, organizing and making sense of the data will require the services of a real estate expert.

For example, you may find a low sales price published for a home in your community. What you don't know is that the home was rife with mold, half the roof was missing, and the septic field was backing up into the basement. REALTORS® should know this kind of information. In fact, the best ones know a great deal about many of the properties within their areas of expertise. They can help you analyze and digest the information and then effectively apply it to your property.

If the agent you pick <u>can't</u> do this for you, find another one. A true expert looks at sales, homes that are currently on the market, homes that did not sell, and the current real estate demand and pricing trends. With that information in hand you'll not only have a good handle on what buyers want, but you will also know what they don't want. That information will help you put together the best package (see the next chapter of this book).

Macro and Micro Trends

It's important to look at both the macro and micro markets impacting your property's value. For instance, your home may be located in a zip code that buyers deem to be "prestigious," even though it's not specifically situated in a high-end neighborhood. Being in that zip code may work to your advantage when it comes time to market your home.

By starting with the big picture (for instance, the city, township, or village) and then working your way down to smaller factors (the zip code level, and then further down to the peer group for your house, specific subdivision, and so forth) you can come up with an excellent way to package your home for sale. With this information in hand, you'll be able to price your home for the fastest sale and avoid grappling with the myriad pricing issues mentioned in this chapter.

Lowering Your Price

Unless your property is unique, or the buyer base for it is extremely small, your first few weeks should produce respectable showing activity. Ideally, you should have had an offer or multiple offers within that first 30-day period. A fair rule of thumb is that an offer should be the result of approximately every 10 showings, although that is no guarantee and it may fluctuate for your home and market. If that has not happened, it may well be time to revisit the price.

> If you miss the pricing variable from the beginning, regroup quickly! You may need to lower the price. Spend more time digesting the data, showing activity, and feedback comments, all which are critically important.

While some complaints can't be changed (like floor plan or neighborhood), multiple comments regarding price (namely, the fact that it's too high) will tell you what the market thinks about your asking price.

The best way to deal with this is by making a smart adjustment before more time progresses. Put on your buyer's hat and ask yourself if you like to overpay for things. If the answer is no, then now is the time to lower the price.

Now that you have a good handle on the very important topic of pricing your home, let's take a look at how to put together a great sales package for your property so you can win!

"Action is the foundational key to all success." –
Pablo Picasso

Chapter Five: Package

If you do everything else correctly, but if the real estate professional that you selected does not promote the house properly, then you are not maximizing this process. When interviewing REALTORS®, make sure the one you choose has a very strong marketing plan and a strategy to get your home sold!

When working for sellers, REALTORS® are responsible for many different tasks and are paid a commission by the seller from the sales proceeds. Marketing the property; getting it sold; and looking out for, protecting, and promoting the best interests of the seller are the three main duties that a good REALTOR® handles for homeowners. Here are just a few of the major tasks that he or she will take on:

- **Create a market snapshot:** The agent will thoroughly inspect your home and outline all the important features and upgrades. He or she will also help determine the Fair Market Value of your property via a detailed, written analysis.

- **Prepare a written home enhancement proposal and come up with a budget for it.** This report will include the recommended repairs and improvements that will help sell your property for the highest price. Key items on this "to do" list will include steps to create curb appeal, and both interior and exterior staging suggestions.

- **Prepare and submit accurate information to the Multiple Listing Service (MLS).** This step will also include photographing your property for both the MLS and for website submissions. Hopefully the agent you select incorporates the services of a professional photographer and videographer.

- **Promote the listing, photos, and videos online.** The top REALTORS® use their own websites, their corporate/franchise sites, national listing sites like REALTOR.com, Zillow, Trulia, and Yahoo Real Estate, and video sites like YouTube to promote your property to a huge audience of national and international buyers. Most are also using social networking sites like Facebook, Twitter, and LinkedIn to actively promote their listings.

- **Use yard signs, lockboxes, brochures, 24-hour toll-free calling, QR codes, property flyers, and other materials to create more promotional opportunities.** Your REALTOR® will be your best friend and advocate during the entire selling process – from the time you sign that listing agreement until you walk away from the closing table with a check in your hand!

Your REALTOR® will also help you negotiate contracts, handle all paperwork related to the sale, connect you with the necessary professionals (home inspectors, appraisers, etc.) to get the property sold, and even navigate any challenges that may surface during the selling period.

An invaluable member of your team, your REALTOR® is well worth the minimal percentage of your total sales price that you'll pay in commissions.

Packaging for Success

By now you have planned your move and gone over the motivations behind it. You've hired a great REALTOR®, staged your home for sale (either on your own or preferably with the help of a professional stager), possibly even made improvements and upgrades if they were warranted, prepared your property for maximum results, and worked with your REALTOR® to price your home properly.

Now it's time to pull all of these elements together into a neat package. The house has to be packaged and relevant. Relevant means different things at different points in history. Whatever your particular timeframe and market conditions are, when you start competing against other homes, yours MUST be relevant.

Preparing a home for sale is a lot like wrapping a beautiful holiday gift. As the giver, you may know firsthand that the gift inside the package is terrific, but if you don't present it in a compelling way there's no way the recipient will know just how wonderful the package's contents are (until it's open, of course). Real estate is similar: if you don't package your home properly, no one will know what a great value it is.

This is why builders don't let their model homes sit empty. They have everything packaged – right down to the fake food posed on plates in the breakfast nook – that can be shown off, including the most expensive upgrade options. The homes are packaged for you to appreciate and act on. They are also packaged for their profitability; your house should not be looked upon any differently.

As the owner of an existing home you should take the same approach that someone looking to have an impact at the holidays would use. A few simple yet intentional touches will make your property shine – just like a certified pre-owned car. Apply the same mentality to the sale of your home and you'll be able to sell it at the highest possible price, based on the property's "perceived value."

On the topic of certified, pre-owned cars, James Bell, editor and publisher of Intellichoice, says, "You may pay a little more in the beginning…plus there's the added benefit of peace of mind, and that's hard to put a price on."

Bell also states that buyers can pay as much as $2,700 more for a certified pre-owned car as compared to a used car.

Taking that certified pre-owned car example a step further, consider the fact that the dealership makes a minimal front-end investment to secure a premium sales price.

As a home seller, why not invest a similar, minimal amount of money on the front end to realize a larger return at the closing table? Do this by securing a pre-sale inspection, addressing any and all reported items, providing the potential homebuyer with the inspection and repair information, and throwing in a home warranty (and, maybe even a pre-sale appraisal).

Your inspection can include environmental items like radon, air quality, well and septic inspections (with septic pumping), and water lab tests.

> Now you have a deficit-free home that comes with a warranty and that is visually appealing, priced properly, and quite frankly crushes the competing homes in both value and style. Combine a buyer's peace of mind with something they are emotionally connecting to and you will always be able to get a higher sales price.

These upfront offers will be extremely attractive to buyers and will increase the odds that you get the asking price for your home. The market may command, for example, $260,000 for a home that was valued at $250,000 before the certified pre-owned approach.

The better news is that it may only take about $2,000 out-of-pocket to earn that additional $10,000 – isn't that worth it? Of course it is. Few, if any, investing options offer that kind of return. And even if this is only half-correct, you still more than doubled your investment. I don't know about you but I'll take that kind of return any day!

It's important to note that this aspect of the sales process revolves around "perceived value." The higher the perceived value in the consumer's eyes, the higher the profit (or, if you have negative equity in your home, the check you need to bring to the closing table will be smaller).

Here's another important note to keep in mind: If you are in a situation where negative equity is present to the point of needing to do a short sale, an investment in any home may obviously not be possible. In fact, this likely isn't the route to take if the property will be positioned on the distressed market.

Be sure to put on your buyer's hat and look at the situation from his or her perspective. Consider how competing properties are being presented and marketed (both online and offline) and prepare a game plan that's focused on winning.

Look at some of the currently listed properties in person. This may change your perspective and help you position your own home in a better, more attractive light. Your goal is to WOW consumers and get them interested in your home – much like the pre-owned car salesman is bent on attracting buyers with a certified, pre-owned car.

If your property is in a municipality that requires an inspection and/or a certificate of occupancy, taking care of these tasks on the front-end for the buyer – and making it known to would-be buyers – will be another feather in your cap. These efforts will add value to the house and likely increase the size of the check you get at closing.

Furthermore, appliances can be a big deal to some buyers. In fact, just recently I was in a few homes, two of which were newly remodeled and gorgeous. But there were no appliances in the homes. That could swing the buyer toward a home that is fully stocked with appliances.

Reaping the Rewards

Right now you may be wondering what you can do to get the highest profit from a home that's not quite ready to show to the rest of the world yet.

Nothing will cost you more money than saying and believing the statement, "I'll just leave my home how it is and let the buyer deal with it so they can then have what they want."

You, your REALTOR®, and your home stager will work in concert to prep your home for sale. Part of that includes a market snapshot that's complete with real-world data that reflects what is selling, what is under contract, what is available, what the market doesn't want, and the seller's budget.

The key is to figure out which investments should be made upfront to spruce up and/or repair the property with the goal of netting the highest possible sales price.

Getting Your Home "Retail Ready"

Kyle Brown, vice president of London-based luxury clothing manufacturer Eskandar, says that years ago when he started in the clothing business, a retail executive said to him: You make or break a sale in the first 10 steps a customer takes in a shop. If there isn't enough to draw them in by then, you've lost their attention…and their business.

"After all my years in the high-end, luxury side of retail, one aspect that the business cannot ever take lightly is visual merchandising," says Brown. "Visual merchandising is an art, science, and serious business in the world of retail. Its goal is to not only sell product, but educate the customer."

Here are some important points that Brown shared, and that can be very easily applied to the art of prepping a home for sale in any market conditions:

> As with any other business, there is a plan put in place for visual merchandising in a store. With this, the retailer sets goals of what they want to achieve and sell. From a luxury end, you need to convince customers the product is worth spending top-dollar for. To achieve this you must connect with a client. You have to know your shopper and your demographic.

From a retail standpoint, your space has to be shoppable. It's important to keep the look and feel simple. Stores can't overdo displays with too many props or merchandise. You can walk into a nice department store that you know has lower prices than anywhere else, but if the merchandise is piled up, thrown everywhere, and too disorderly to make sense of, you're less likely to spend much time in that store, as shopping just becomes too difficult.

"Whatever the product is that you want to highlight, it needs to be easy to see and inviting," says Brown. "Eye appeal is crucial and translates into sales." There are all sorts of enhancements that can be used to draw a customer's attention to an area. These can be anything from lighting, wall décor, relaxing music, fresh flowers, and even the right wall color.

All of this is very important because customers often spend more when they're in an environment they feel comfortable in. Like anything else, store atmosphere is critical and retailers spend millions of dollars every year to improve this.

Lighting, for example, is very significant. You have to use it to your advantage. A retailer wants to make sure that their new, key merchandise for the season is front and forward and well lit. Whereas, you may notice, when you walk in a store the sale merchandise can often be pushed to the back corner with less light. Customers feel less comfortable in a darker space versus a shop that's well lit. "We all respond emotionally to visual stimuli, and lighting can make all the difference," says Brown.

This is comparable to the use of light in the home staging process. For instance, a tile backsplash in the kitchen should be set off with some under-cabinet lighting to make it "pop" in online photos. This will help get the prospective buyers through the door to see that glimmering, delightful goodness in person!

In the end, a retailer has to sit back and identify the objectives with each section of a shop. What's there that is most important to highlight? Planning ahead of time is imperative for optimization of a space. It has to be inviting from the first step in, as well as keeping interesting features towards the back of the store to draw the customer in and keep them interested.

Psychologist Jerome Bruner of New York University has described studies that show people only remember 10% of what they hear and 20% of what they read, but about 80% of what they see and do. [1]

In the retail business today, you have to capture the customer's attention immediately in order to compete for their business. "People may shop around more before committing to spend nowadays, but if they're given an impressive store experience, they're more likely to remember that store and continue shopping there," says Brown.

So what does it take to get a home "retail ready" in the same way that high-end clothing manufacturers do to ensure that they are appealing to their customers? The first step is to get into the mind of the buyer. Ask yourself questions like:

---

[1] Paul Martin Lester, "Syntactic Theory of Visual Communication," California State University at Fullerton, 1994-1996.

• What do you want to see, hear, smell, and experience when you walk into the home?
• How should things be organize and categorized?
• Will I be able to personalize this home to my own tastes and preferences?
• What will really make me buy this home?
• Looking around, is this the kind of home that should be selling at a discount?
• Can I picture myself living in this home?

Make your buyers *want* to be in your home and help them picture themselves living in it. An easy way to achieve this is by removing your personal photos and knickknacks. Leave room for the buyer to envision his or her own possessions in the dwelling (since you've already had the property staged, this necessary component has probably already been addressed). De-personalizing your property accomplishes these three key goals:

- First, it allows buyers to picture themselves living in the house;

- Second, buyers don't feel like they are intruding on the owner; and
- Third they will likely stay in the home longer and look around more.

Your goal is to minimize distractions and to make buyers LOVE your home and want to live in it. If your walls are covered with family photos, you can bet the buyers will stare at each one, trying to figure out who is in the photos and not paying much attention to the home that you are trying to sell.

I can't tell you how often I have been showing a home to buyer clients and had them stare at the photos, convinced that they know them somehow, went to school with them, or even used to date them! Yes, I recently had a husband mention – in front of his wife and I – that he used to date the lady in the picture on the wall. Needless to say, that made for an awkward rest of the afternoon. This is living proof that no good can come from having personal photos plastered around a home that's listed for sale.

Putting the Package Together

As you learned in this chapter, there are some specific steps that you can take to position your home as a certified pre-owned property that buyers will flock to and even pay a premium for.

By investing some pre-market time and dollars in staging, pre-inspections, repairs, home warranties, and even an appraisal, you can up the ante even further and give buyers peace of mind that many other sellers won't pay attention to.

> Put yourself in the buyers' shoes. Market your home like a luxury clothier would. You'll be in the best possible position when it comes time to put that "for sale" sign in your front yard. Then, turn that FOR SALE into SOLD, knowing that you did all you could to maximize the proceeds, minimize the market time, and help the housing market and the economy.

As was mentioned at the beginning of this chapter, part of the "packaging" step when selling a home involves exactly how your agent promotes the property. This critical step ties back into the agent's marketing plan and why you hired him or her to begin with. Exactly how this professional will promote your home to the rest of the world is an extremely important aspect of the packaging process and should not be taken lightly.

In the next chapter we'll take a brief look at what you can expect from the sales and showing process, and help you maintain perspective during this stage.

"With ordinary talent and extraordinary perseverance, all things are attainable." –
Thomas Foxwell Buxton

Chapter Six: Persevere

Once that "for sale" sign is staked out in your front yard and your home claims a spot on the local Multiple Listing Service, you'll need to be ready to show your property at any time. Excuses like "I have to clean this weekend," or "We were out late last night and want to sleep in," won't cut it when a buyer wants to see the property in person on a Saturday morning at 9am.

The best way to deal with these intrusions (and over time that's what they'll feel like – trust me!) is to look at the sale of your home as a business proposition. Take the emotions out of it and view it solely as a decision you've made to *increase your wealth through the sale of your home* (or, as in the case of a distressed sale, to get out from under a financial burden).

Also understand that it's entirely possible that the buyers who didn't get a chance to see your property upon request will forget to come back, and may commit to purchasing another home before they even think about your home again. Don't miss out on these opportunities!

So what does this mean? It means that your home will become a **product for sale** versus a roof over your head. Dinners may be disrupted, beds will need to be made every morning (preferably with hospital corners), and clothing, toys, and other clutter will need to be kept to a bare minimum.

It also means that you should be prepared at any moment to accommodate potential buyers. Of course there are some exceptions to the rule – such as holidays – but for the most part you should assume that buyers will want to see your home on any given day and at any hour. Be prepared for this because it <u>will</u> happen.

If the "any time" showings become overwhelming just remember a rule of thumb that we use in the real estate industry: the more showings, the better. The more showings, the more interest and the better the odds that you'll get an offer on your home. Ideally, a high level of activity results in higher demand, multiple offers, and a premium price paid.

In the final chapter of this book we will wind up discussion of the home-selling process and leave you with some sage advice on how to approach the sale of your own home.

"Happiness lies in the joy of achievement and the thrill of creative effort." –

Franklin D. Roosevelt

Chapter Seven: Post-Game

Thanks to the book you're holding in your hands you are now equipped with the knowledge you need to win the selling game in any type of market conditions. Please share this book with anyone who will be selling their property soon – consider it the equivalent of giving them a large check!

> The most important lesson to take away from this book is that you should never leave a transaction and transition of this size to chance.

For many, the sale or purchase of a home is the largest transaction that they'll ever be involved in. And even if you don't fall into this category, it's still a sizeable decision, so don't talk yourself into believing that 20-year-old green floral kitchen wallpaper will be "changed by the buyer!"

A small investment in replacing that 20-year-old green floral kitchen wallpaper may very well add to your bottom line, get the right buyer faster, and with ultimately less effort. These and other considerations (regardless of how inconsequential they may seem to you) will go a long way in ensuring that you get top dollar for your property.

Having spent over a decade of my life so far in the real estate industry, I can tell you that a strong, healthy, housing market benefits *everyone.* Regardless of where you are located, my goal is to help build strong households, neighborhoods, cities, and regions.

By using this playbook as your guide – and by investing effort, thought, time, and money into your home-selling journey – you will be contributing to this overall goal while lining your own pockets with more money than you would have on your own.

I wish you well – and happy, profitable selling!

www.ingramcontent.com/pod-product-compliance
Lightning Source LLC
Chambersburg PA
CBHW071622170526
45166CB00003B/1160